Pebble®
Plus

Investigate the Seasons

Let's Look at Summer

Revised Edition

Sarah L Schuette

raintree

a Capstone company — publishers for children

Raintree is an imprint of Capstone Global Library Limited, a company incorporated in England and Wales having its registered office at 264 Banbury Road, Oxford, OX2 7DY – Registered company number: 6695582

www.raintree.co.uk
myorders@raintree.co.uk

Editorial credits
Sarah Bennett, designer; Tracy Cummins, media researcher, Laura Manthe, production specialist

Photo credits
Alamy: F. Rauschenbach, 11; Shutterstock: Artens, 21, ConstantinosZ, Cover, Fer Gregory, 13, Garsya, 3, LazarenkoD, 7, Liubou Yasiukovich, Cover Design Element, majeczka, 5, martin33, 17, Marty Nelson, 9, Sergey Kotelnikov, 19, vblinov, 15, WDG Photo, 1

Printed and bound in India

ISBN 978 1 4747 5660 0
22 21 20 19 18
10 9 8 7 6 5 4 3 2 1

British Library Cataloguing in Publication Data

A full catalogue record for this book is available from the British Library.

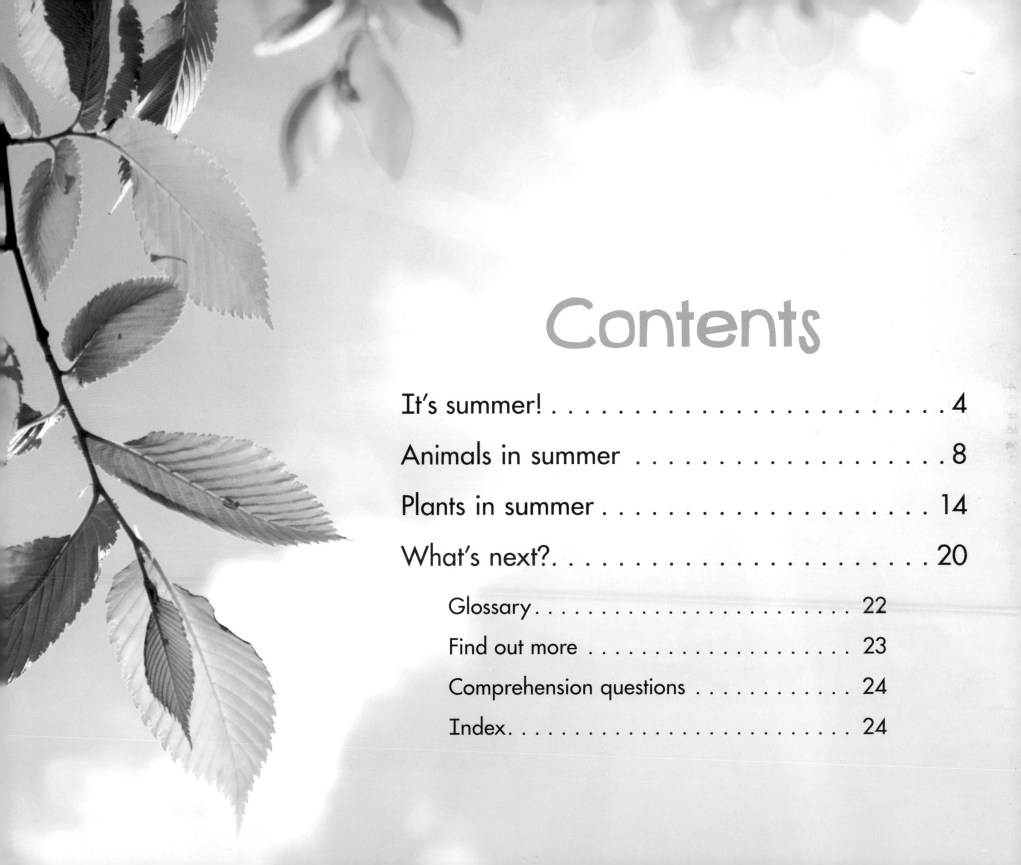

Contents

It's summer!

How do you know

it's summer?

The temperature rises.

It's the warmest season.

The sun shines high

in the sky.

Summer days are

the longest of the year.

Animals in summer

What do animals do
in summer?
Deer rest in the shade
to keep cool.

Tadpoles grow

into young frogs.

They find lots of bugs to eat.

Fireflies light up

on summer nights.

They flash to find mates.

Plants in summer

What happens to plants

in summer?

Trees are full

of green leaves.

Plump cherries hang
from branches.
They are a tasty
summer treat.

What's next?

The weather gets colder.

Summer is over.

What season comes next?

Glossary

mate partner or one of a pair; fireflies flash their lights to attract mates

season one of the four parts of the year; winter, spring, summer and autumn are seasons

shade area out of the sun

tadpole young frog; tadpoles hatch from eggs and swim in water

temperature measure of how hot or cold something is

Find out more

Books

Summer (Seasons), Stephanie Turnbull (Franklin Watts, 2015)

The Seasons (Our Special World), Liz Lennon (Franklin Watts, 2016)

What Can You See in Summer? (Seasons), Sian Smith (Raintree, 2014)

Websites

www.dkfindout.com/uk/earth/seasons
Find out more about the seasons on this website.

www.bbc.co.uk/education/clips/zbdkjxs
Watch this video to see the changes in nature through the seasons.

Comprehension questions

1. What happens to the days during summer?

2. How do deer stay cool in summer?

3. Describe how you stay cool during the season of summer.

Index